THE STORY OF THINGS

Written by Kate Morgan

Illustrations by Joyce Audy Zarins

WALKER AND COMPANY

NEW YORK

To Amber
—K.M.

To my husband, Egils
—J.A.Z.

ACKNOWLEDGMENTS
The author gratefully acknowledges the expertise of the Anthropology Department at UCLA.

ABOUT THE ART

The art for *The Story of Things* was created with washes of Winsor & Newton watercolors and gouaches over Pelikan waterproof brown ink applied with a crowquill pen. The paper used was 140 pound Fabriano cold press.

Once reference material was found, the image was roughed out in pencil, then clarified and extended in ink using nibs of different widths. The watercolor was applied last using sable brushes.

Library of Congress Cataloging-in-Publication Data • Morgan, Kate, The story of things / written by Kate Morgan, illustrated by Joyce Audy Zarins. p. cm. Summary: A brief and general history of inventions from the beginning of humankind to the present. ISBN 0-8027-6918-7. — ISBN 0-8027-6919-5 (reinforced bdg.) 1. Inventions—Juvenile literature. [1. Inventions.] I. Zarins, Joyce Audy, ill. II. Title. T48.M68 1991 609—dc20 90-48165 CIP AC
Printed in Hong Kong • 10 9 8 7 6 5 4 3 2 1

How many of these things could
you live without?

Millions of years ago, people had only earth, water, plants, animals, and fire. They ate berries and nuts, seeds, insects, and birds' eggs.

What's new: 3,500,000 B.C.

fossil footprints of an adult and child from more than 3,000,000 years ago have been found in Africa.

Some people caught small animals with their hands. They found the animal's skin was tough. They couldn't rip it with their teeth. They couldn't tear it with their hands. They had to think of a way to cut the skin. Someone hit one rock against another. The edge chipped and was sharp. People had a tool to use.

What's new: 3,000,000 B.C.

For thousands of years, people used the stone chopper to skin animals, cut flesh, scrape hides, chop wood, and dig roots.

Stone tools

When lightning struck, trees and grasses blazed hot and wild. People were afraid, and for many years they ran away from fire.

In time, a few brave people came back to the warmth and light. Others followed. Some held sticks in the fire.

Now they had fire to use.

What's new: 1,000,000 B.C.

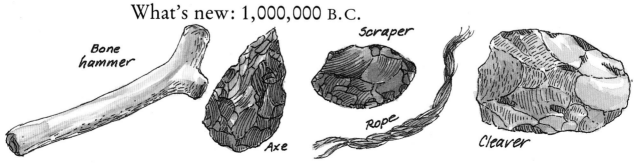

Bone hammer

Axe

Scraper

Rope

Cleaver

People learned they could hunt
bigger animals if they worked together. Teamwork meant people
had to understand each other.
Later the sounds they made became words.

People used fire to drive animals out of caves. People lived in the warm caves until they moved on to new hunting grounds.

People met other people. They showed each other what they had learned.

What's new: 700,000 to 125,000 B.C.

Borer— for making holes

Leather thong for sewing

Bone awl

Stone spear head

Fire making tools

They told their children . . .

And their children's
children . . .

And their children's children's
children didn't have to discover
everything for themselves. They
could think of new things.

Over many thousands of years, people became expert hunters. They had time to think about how they looked, so they decorated themselves.

They noticed what was around them. Someone saw that the dirt around a fire was hard. In time, people learned to mix dirt with water to make clay. They shaped the clay and put it by the fire to harden.

What's new: 100,000 to 10,000 B.C.

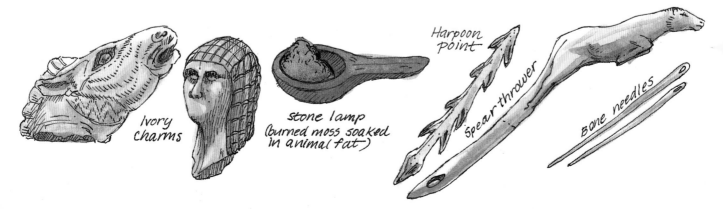

Ivory charms

stone lamp
(burned moss soaked in animal fat)

Harpoon Point

Spear thrower

Bone needles

When animals were hard to find, people wished for food. They believed that painting a picture of their wish would make it come true.

Artist's tools

Mortar + pestle

shell to hold color

scraper to spread color

"crayons" made of charcoal, ochre and colored clay mixed with animal fat

stone palette

Hollow bone to blow on powdered color

Snail Shells

stones with etched designs

Jewelry

Painted Pebbles

making pottery

Dugout canoe

thatched roof covered with mud

oven

irrigation ditch

clay and mud walls

weaving   calling

hiding

herding

grain storage

playing on seesaw

Grinding grain

playing house

fixing roof

In search of food, some people hollowed out logs. Using wooden paddles, they crossed the water to hunt animals in other lands.

Some people returned to where they had found food before. They saw new grasses had grown.

In time, people discovered grasses and plants had grown from seeds that had fallen to the ground.

Where weather was warm and water flowed, plants grew quickly.

trading

Bricks drying

What's new: 10,000 to 5,000 B.C.

wheat

Barley

Rice

Person grinding grain

Storage jars

Oven Doll-House

Pottery tray-ridged for removing grain husks

Grindstones

Antler sickle

sharp bits of stone

Fishing

grain

Making baskets

playing catch

Digging

Sowing

Hoeing

heating oven for bread

Milking

Now some people grew their own food. Now they could live in one place. Groups settled along rivers and seacoasts, on lake shores and islands. People worked together to dig ditches for irrigating crops.

Hunters brought the young of wild animals home. People fed the animals, and they stayed close.

Now that people didn't have to carry their belongings, they began to make and collect things.

With more people living together, each person could do the kind of work he liked best.

People traded with each other. To keep records of trades, they cut marks into sticks.

spindle

wood →

spun wool →

clay whorl →

weaving loom

wool

Basket

Better arrows

Brick

Pottery spoon

Fish hook

In some areas, people found a bright hard metal in the ground. Curious, they put the metal on a rock in an oven. The metal melted.

When the oven cooled, people saw the metal had hardened in the shape of the rock. Some people called the metal *kypris*. Later kypris became known as copper. It was soft and chipped easily.

Crafting pots

molding metal

What's new: 5,000 to 3,000 B.C.

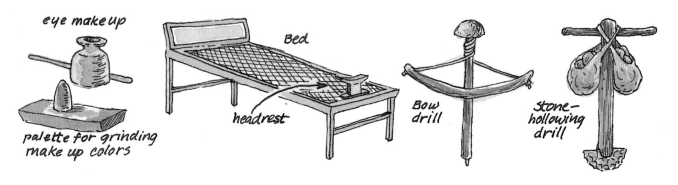

eye makeup

palette for grinding make up colors

Bed

headrest

Bow drill

stone-hollowing drill

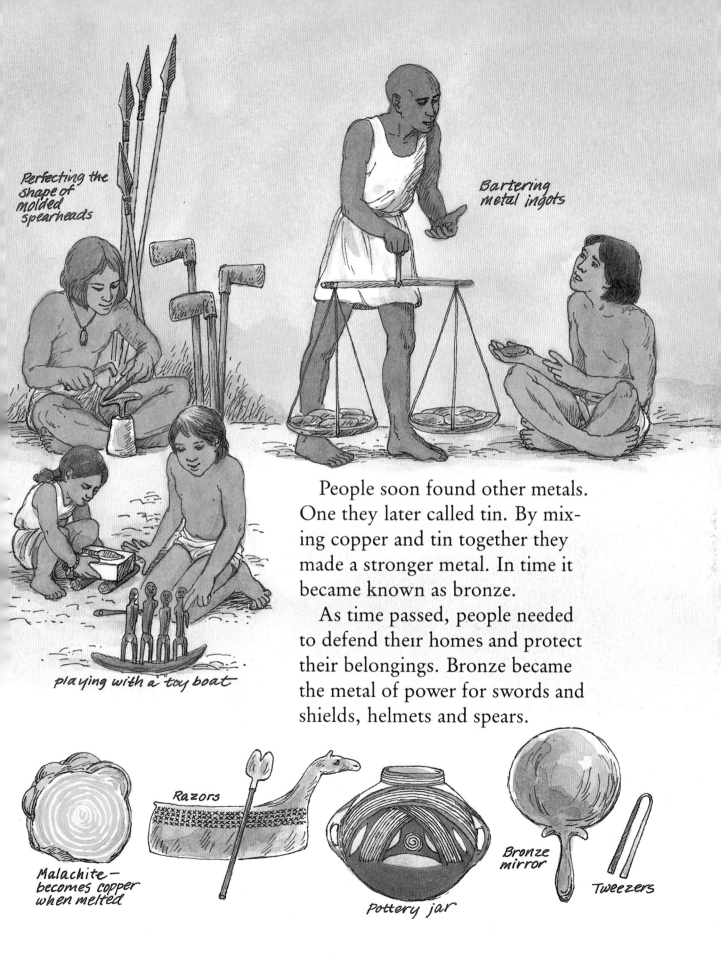

Perfecting the shape of molded spearheads

Bartering metal ingots

playing with a toy boat

People soon found other metals. One they later called tin. By mixing copper and tin together they made a stronger metal. In time it became known as bronze.

As time passed, people needed to defend their homes and protect their belongings. Bronze became the metal of power for swords and shields, helmets and spears.

Malachite — becomes copper when melted

Razors

Pottery jar

Bronze mirror

Tweezers

Villages became towns. In some, priests wanted temples, the rich wanted bigger houses, and kings wanted tombs.

People needed a way to carry heavy loads. They used the trunks of trees as rollers. Someone shortened the trunks. The first carts moved only forward and back. To turn a corner, the driver picked up the cart and turned it.

The oldest known wheels were from Ur.

Logs as rollers

Wheelbarrows— the first wheeled carriers

The first carts

What's new: 3,000 to 2,000 B.C.

Hair curlers

Popcorn

Ebony (Black wood)

Umbrellas

Domestic Cats and Dogs

People thought of ways to improve their work. They made pottery wheels, kilns, and better weaving looms.

Most people wanted more things. Merchants traveled from one area to another over oceans and deserts, mountains and valleys, trading grains and flax, gold and gems, cotton, ivory, wood, and copper.

Merchants unloading

Carrying water in jars

Drawing water with a shaduf.

Making Pottery

Weaving

Spinning wool

Barber at work

Drilling holes

making pictures in clay

Playing Serpent—the oldest known Egyptian game.

Playing catch with a ball of leather stuffed with straw.

Toys with moving parts

shoes

Cotton

Animal branding iron

In time, towns grew into cities. Taxes were collected. Soldiers were recruited. Riches were brought from other lands. Records needed to be kept.

People drew pictures on wet clay.

Instead of carrying knowledge in their heads, or remembering the stories of their parents and grandparents, people could write down what they knew: how to work with metal, how to weave, how to build a house.

People could also begin to know what was happening to them. They could ask questions. Is this city getting bigger? Do we need more crops? Am I getting older?

What's new: 2,000 to 1,800 B.C.

Papyrus reeds

peel rind

slice

Making Egyptian paper

2 layers of papyrus strips

flat stone

polishing stone

mallet

Cover cloth

1. Cover papyrus with cloth
2. Beat with mallet for an hour or two
3. Press under a heavy weight
4. Polish with a rounded stone
5. Glue end to end to make a scroll

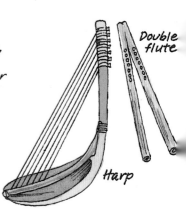

Double flute

Harp

As the sun moved across the sky, a person looked at the changing shadow on the ground. He drew marks in the dirt and made a way to tell time.

People saw that certain things happened at the same time each year. Green leaves sprouted, birds flew overhead, rivers flooded.

They knew it was time to plant. They made a calendar to mark the seasons.

Musical clappers

Drum

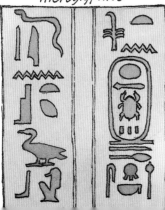

Hieroglyphics

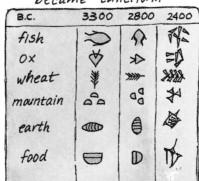

Picture writing on clay became cuneiform

B.C.	3300	2800	2400
fish			
ox			
wheat			
mountain			
earth			
food			

Skiis—wood covered with Reindeer skin (Northern countries)

Many people lived in the world now.

Some people robbed. Some people murdered. Some people damaged other peoples' land.

Wise leaders made rules:

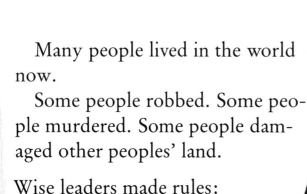

IF A MAN HAS STOLEN AN OX, A SHEEP, AN ASS OR A PIG OR A BOAT, IF IT BELONGS TO A GOD OR IF IT BELONGS TO A PALACE, HE SHALL PAY THIRTY-FOLD.

IF A MAN HAS BROKEN THE LIMB OF ANOTHER MAN WITH A WEAPON IN A FIGHT, HE SHALL PAY ONE MINA OF SILVER.

What's new: 1,800 to 600 B.C.

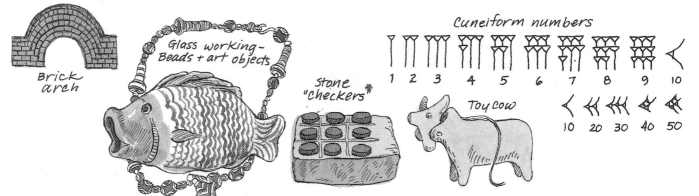

Brick arch

Glass working- Beads + art objects

Stone "Checkers"

Cuneiform numbers

1	2	3	4	5	6	7	8	9	10

10	20	30	40	50

Toy cow

The more crowded cities became, the more things people needed. Farmers and carpenters, shipbuilders and blacksmiths, jewelers, cooks, and bakers, shoemakers and miners, tanners, potters, weavers, teachers, scribes, gardeners, tax collectors, and priests all needed a way to keep better records.

Pictures became symbols, symbols became an alphabet.

Other symbols became numbers.

safety pin

water clock

Etruscan ink bottle with a 26 letter alphabet on it.

ABCDEFIⴲⴲIK

LMNⴲOPMⵕ

PSTVSⴲV

Gold coins

People asked questions about the world around them.

What keeps the stars in the sky?

What causes day and night?

Why does the moon change shape?

Astronomers made an instrument to measure the altitudes of the stars and planets. They measured the height of the sun at midday, and knew the moon's distance from the earth.

Plato's model of the universe

quadrant

wax tablet "notebook"

armillary sphere

Ptolemy used an astrolabe to measure the height of a star.

What's new: 600 B.C. to 1200 A.D.

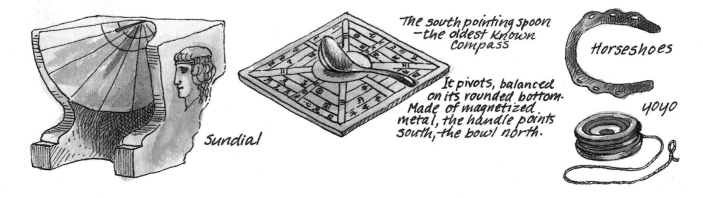

Sundial

The south pointing spoon —the oldest known compass

It pivots, balanced on its rounded bottom. Made of magnetized metal, the handle points south, the bowl north.

Horseshoes

yoyo

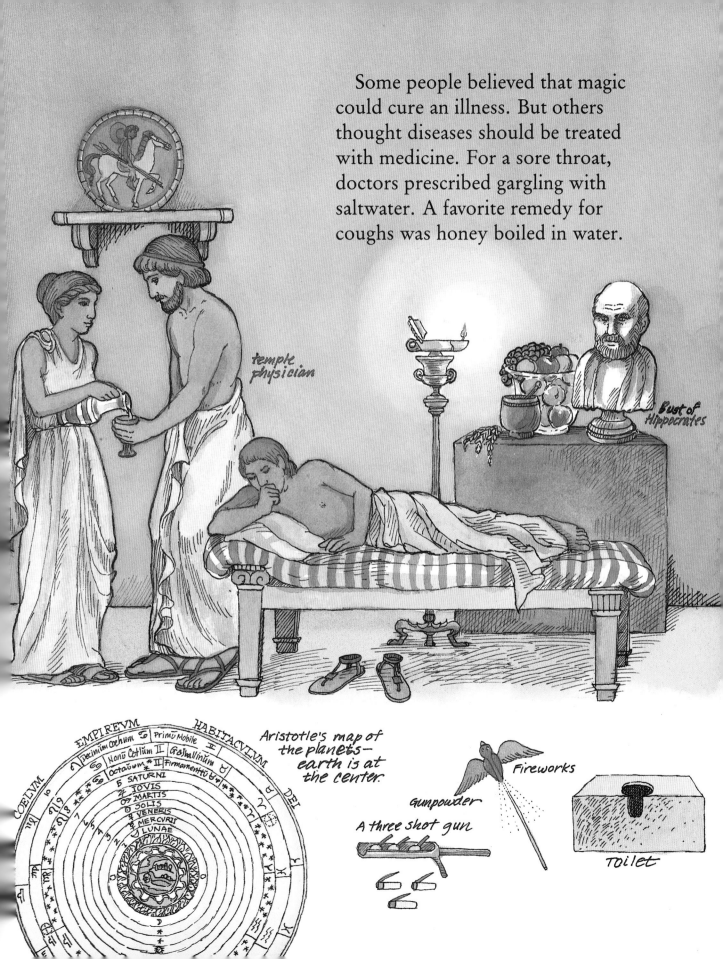

Some people believed that magic could cure an illness. But others thought diseases should be treated with medicine. For a sore throat, doctors prescribed gargling with saltwater. A favorite remedy for coughs was honey boiled in water.

temple physician

Bust of Hippocrates

Aristotle's map of the planets—earth is at the center.

Fireworks

Gunpowder

A three shot gun

Toilet

In the next few centuries, an explorer proved that the earth was round, a microscope showed life in a drop of water, and the telescope expanded people's ideas about the universe.

The more people learned, the more they invented—eyeglasses in 1300; the printing press in 1455; pencils in 1565; the microscope in 1590; a thermometer in 1592; the telescope in 1608; a calculator in 1642; magazines in 1663; croissants in 1683; and the piano in 1709.

Everything was made by hand.

printing press

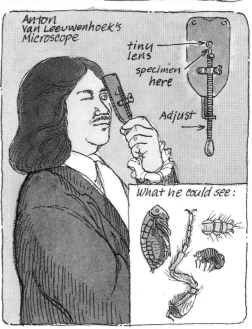

Anton Van Leeuwenhoek's Microscope

tiny lens

specimen here

Adjust

What he could see:

Two of Galileo's telescopes

Pencil

Rubber ball

Eyeglasses

What's new: 1300 to 1700

Newton's steam car

spinning wheel

waterwheels

windmill

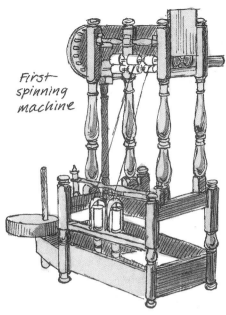

First spinning machine

Before newspapers, town criers shouted the news.

Before post offices, a letter took ten days to go the 400 miles from London to Edinburgh.

People were in a hurry, and they invented machines.

Now machines did the work of people. The world would never be the same again.

New! steam carriage

First mechanical loom

First road Locomotive

What's new: 1700 to 1800

Cotton gin

Hot air balloon— man's first flight

Rail trolley

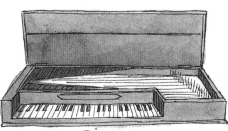

Piano

Steam power sped people over oceans and across continents. It plowed through fields, tilling soil and harvesting crops. Steam hammered iron into steel and drove machines to make more machines to build cities.

What's new: 1800 to 1850

Friction matches

The first stethoscope: Rene Läennec got the idea from watching children at play. One held a long piece of wood to his ear, the other tapped on a pin stuck in the other end. The sound was carried by the wood.

POSTAGE ONE PENNY

stamps

canned food

Now time was money. Electricity powered the world and life took a turn for the faster with automatic washing machines and electric stoves, plug-in irons and vacuum cleaners.

Communications were speeded up with telephones and typewriters. Zippers replaced buttons. People rode elevators and danced to music on the phonograph. The electric light turned night into a new world.

What's new: 1850 to 1900

Electric Light

Elevator

Safety Lock

Ice maker

Camera

Now people
. . . send written messages at the
     speed of sound
. . . fly more than 3,000 miles in
     less than four hours
. . . put satellites into space
that can see a tree, hear a voice,
track a disaster on earth, and
relay
information
in three hundred,
fourteen-volume encyclopedias with
1,200 pages in each volume and
2,000 words on each page,
in
one
second.

What's new today:

Automatic teller

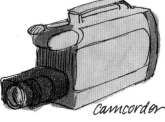

Camcorder

Solar power

Microwave

LCD's

People are exploring other planets, other galaxies, and will make more things to shape new worlds.

Remote control

Robot

Radar

Supersonic Travel

Things from the past have led to things people use today. What new things do you think people will use in the future?